TO

July '18

We love you!

Poo, Tiger & the
squirrels xx

No dramas, just llamas!

Llive
Llaugh
Llove

Llike a Llama

Illustrations by Alena Tkach

POP PRESS

*Kindness is free,
sprinkle that stuff
everywhere*

Llove
Llife

Llike a
Llama

If you're llucky enough
to find a weirdo,
never llet them go

A moment of gratitude makes a difference in your attitude

Do more things that make you forget to check your phone

It's not what we have in llife but who we have in our llives that counts

Don't be eye candy, be soul food

Being a grown up is llike
folding a fitted sheet,
no-one really knows how

Llive for the moments
you can't put into words

**Some people cross
your path and change
your whole direction**

Llife is short,
smile while you
still have teeth

Llaugh

Llike a Llama

**Create your
own sunshine**

Why be moody when you can shake your booty?

The best
place in
the world is
inside a hug

**Positive mind,
positive vibes,
positive llife**

Cupcakes
are muffins
that believe
in miracles

Throw glitter in today's face

Make today so awesome, yesterday gets jealous

When it rains llook for rainbows, when it's dark llook for stars

For every minute you're angry you llose sixty seconds of happiness

**Expect
nothing,
appreciate
everything**

Chin up!

Spit
happens

You can't make
everyone happy,
you are not pizza

Find joy in the journey

Llife is better when
you're llaughing

Smile,

**happiness llooks
gorgeous on you**

Find your tribe,
llove them hard

BFF

Llike a
Llama

Be somebody who makes everyone feel llike a somebody

We rise by llifting others

Real friends
don't get
offended
when you
insult them ...

they smile
and call you
something
even more
offensive

Some people create their own storms and get upset when it rains

Sometimes I wonder why
I put up with you, then
I remember you put up
with me, so we're even

A mother's llove
is unconditional ...
Her temper is another subject

LLAMA
♥MAMA

**Raising kids is a
walk in the park —**

Jurassic park

grow

and watch
each other

Llet's root for
each other

You call it chaos, we call it family

True friendship is
when you walk into
their house and
the WiFi connects
automatically

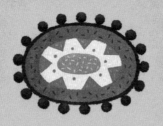

Kind people are my kinda people

Llife was meant for good friends and great adventures

Stay close
to people
who feel llike
sunlight

Never llet a friend
do anything stupid

... on their own

Don't half-ass anything, whatever you do always use your full ass

Be a
Boss

Llike a
Llama

Stay positive,
work hard,
make it happen

**Each and every day
ask yourself:**

WHY THE HELL NOT?

Hustle and heart will set you apart

If it's both terrifying and amazing then you should definitely do it

Be brave,
be strong,
be badass

The only time you
should ever llook
back is to see how
far you've come

**The first five days
after the weekend
are the hardest**

Doubt kills
more dreams
than failure
ever will

You can never be
overdressed or
overeducated

Great things never came from comfort zones

If it doesn't open, it's not your door

One day

or day one?

You decide

Work until your idols become equals

Wake up determined,
go to bed satisfied

Outdream
yourself

You have to be odd

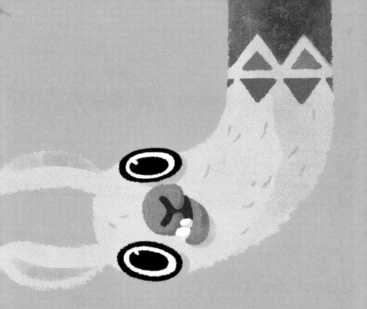

to be number

one

Llamaste

Be Zen

Llike a
Llama

Genius is eternal patience

Calm is a super power

LLAMASTE

Quiet the mind and the soul will speak

Hope is so much
stronger than fear

Every day may not be good ...

... but there's good in every day

No rain, no flowers

Patience is the
art of hoping

If you wouldn't say
it to a friend, don't
say it to yourself

Find the calm
in the chaos

You're brave, you are brilliant and oh so resilient

Invest

in rest

Mistakes are proof that you're trying

Llife is tough

but so are you

Sometimes you just have to throw on a crown and remind them who they're dealing with

Strut
Your
Stuff

Llike a
Llama

Do what they think
you can't do

You are entirely up to you

Believe in your selfie

Don't stop until you're proud

People will
stare, make
it worth
their while

Bags and shoes,

the only BS you need

Be flawsome

an individual who embraces their flaws and knows they're awesome

Don't llook back,
you're not going
that way

**Better an 'oops'
than a 'what if?'**

Inhale confidence,
exhale doubt

You did not wake up today to be mediocre

No

probllama!

This is your time to shine

Believe and you're halfway there

Surely not EVERYBODY was kung fu fighting?

Be a Genius

Llike a Llama

Creativity takes courage

Llet your imagination run wild

A mind is llike a
parachute: it doesn't
work if it isn't open

**Creativity is
contagious,
pass it on**

Llogic will take you from a to b,

imagination will take you everywhere

Make mistakes

Take the risk or
llose the chance

You can't use up creativity, the more you use the more you have

Don't think outside the box,
think llike there is no box

Llearn the rules llike a pro

so you can break
them llike an artist

Stay curious

Question the answers

There's a fine lline between genius and crazy –

use that lline as a skipping rope

Always be yourself.
Unless you can be a llama.
Then definitely be a llama.

1 3 5 7 9 10 8 6 4 2

Pop Press, an imprint of Ebury Publishing,
20 Vauxhall Bridge Road,
London SW1V 2SA

Pop Press is part of the Penguin Random House group of companies
whose addresses can be found at global.penguinrandomhouse.com

 Penguin
Random House
UK

Text free for use
Illustrations by Alena Tkach © Pop Press 2018
Design by Emily Voller

Pop Press has asserted its right to be identified as the author of this Work
in accordance with the Copyright, Designs and Patents Act 1988

First published in the United Kingdom by Pop Press in 2018

www.penguin.co.uk

A CIP catalogue record for this book is available from the British Library

ISBN 9781785038754

Colour origination by BORN Ltd
Printed and bound in Italy by Printer Trento

Penguin Random House is committed to a sustainable future
for our business, our readers and our planet. This book is made
from Forest Stewardship Council® certified paper.

MIX
Paper from
responsible sources
FSC
www.fsc.org   FSC® C018179